Mysterious You

Aha!

The most interesting book you'll ever read about intelligence

Written by Trudee Romanek

Illustrated by Rose Cowles

Kids Can Press

To Graham, for always asking "Why?" — T.R.

My sincere thanks to Dr. Lise Eliot of The Chicago Medical School and Dr. Stanley Coren of the University of British Columbia, two experts in their fields who willingly reviewed this manuscript. My appreciation also to John De Oliveira of Cycorp Inc., Athey Educational for their IQ questions, and to Susan, my good friend, who just happens to be a fantastic resource as well.

As always, thanks to the talented trio of Liz MacLeod, Marie Bartholomew and Rose Cowles, who turn my simple words into the dashing book you hold in your hands.

Text © 2004 Trudee (Tomlinson) Romanek
Illustrations © 2004 Rose Cowles

Kids Can Press acknowledges the financial support of the Government of Ontario, through the Ontario Media Development Corporation's Ontario Book Initiative; the Ontario Arts Council; the Canada Council for the Arts; and the Government of Canada, through the BPIDP, for our publishing activity.

Published in Canada by
Kids Can Press Ltd.
29 Birch Avenue
Toronto, ON M4V 1E2

Published in the U.S. by
Kids Can Press Ltd.
2250 Military Road
Tonawanda, NY 14150

www.kidscanpress.com

Edited by Elizabeth MacLeod
Designed by Marie Bartholomew
Printed in Hong Kong, China, by Wing King Tong

The hardcover edition of this book is smyth sewn casebound.
The paperback edition of this book is limp sewn with a drawn-on cover.

CM 04 0 9 8 7 6 5 4 3 2 1
CM PA 04 0 9 8 7 6 5 4 3 2 1

Tests on page 19 are courtesy of Athey Educational, Tibthorpe, Driffield, East Yorkshire, and appear here with permission.

National Library of Canada Cataloguing in Publication Data

Romanek, Trudee
    Aha! : the most interesting book you'll ever read about intelligence / written by Trudee Romanek ; illustrated by Rose Cowles.

(Mysterious you)
Includes index.

ISBN 1-55337-485-1 (bound).   ISBN 1-55337-569-6 (pbk.)

1. Intellect — Juvenile literature. 2. Learning, Psychology of — Juvenile literature. I. Cowles, Rose, 1967– II. Title. III. Series: Mysterious you (Toronto, Ont.)

BF431.R64 2004   j153.9   C2003-903379-1

Kids Can Press is a *Corus*™ Entertainment company

Contents

Your Smart Brain   4

A Head for Learning   8

Measuring Up   18

Making the Most of Your Smarts   28

Searching for Intelligence   34

Index   40

Your Smart Brain

Stephen Hawking has amyotrophic lateral sclerosis, or ALS — a disease that means he can't control his muscles. ALS keeps Hawking's body in a wheelchair, but not his mind. Many people consider Hawking the most intelligent person alive today.

He's a cosmologist — a person who tries to figure out the mind-boggling mysteries of what the universe is like, when it began and how and when it's likely to end. He's already changed many experts' views on what black holes are and what happens inside them.

Hawking can tackle this difficult work because he's very intelligent. And his impressive intelligence comes from his brain, just as your intelligence comes from your brain — that wrinkly lump of squishy, pinkish tissue inside your head.

Without your intelligence, you wouldn't know a turnip from a toucan. You couldn't learn your name or tie your shoelaces. And you definitely wouldn't be able to read this book.

What Is Intelligence?

For hundreds of years, people have tried to figure out just what it means to be intelligent. In the late 1800s, one theory was that since we gain all of our knowledge through our senses—sight, hearing, taste, touch and smell—the most intelligent people must be those with the most acute senses.

Now many experts agree that intelligence is not just the information you know or the activities you've learned to do. Instead, it's your ability to use what you know to solve problems, learn new things or change when a situation changes. Intelligence is really about how well you cope in the world.

- In 350 B.C. people believed it was the heart, not the brain, that held our intelligence.

- Your incredible brain can learn and store away as much information as 20 volumes of an encyclopedia.

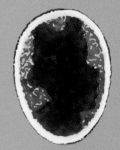

A No-Brainer

You need a brain to be intelligent, right? Maybe not, according to a 1980s report by brain specialist John Lorber. A doctor friend at Sheffield University in England sent a student to Lorber because the doctor had noticed that the student's head was slightly larger than normal.

A brain scan showed that the young man had only a very thin layer of brain tissue where most people have tissue about 4.5 cm (1³⁄₄ in.) thick. Instead of brain, the young man's skull was mostly filled with fluid. And yet he was a top math student.

Lorber looked further and found a group of people who have abnormally small brains but function perfectly well, many with above-average intelligence. For now, no expert can explain how that's possible.

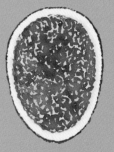

average brain   patient's brain

Starting from Nothing?

Intelligence isn't just about what you know but also how much you can learn. Newborn babies, who can't read or even talk, are still considered very smart because they're such incredible learning machines.

Researchers gave each of a group of one-month-old babies a pacifier to suck on without letting the baby see it. Some pacifiers were smooth. Others were covered in small bumps. Later, the researchers showed each baby a smooth pacifier and a bumpy one. Almost all the babies stared longer at the type of pacifier they'd been sucking on. They could tell just from how it looked which type they'd had in their mouth.

Experiments also show that a newborn baby recognizes his mother's voice. He can even recognize a story that his mother read aloud a number of times during the final weeks before birth.

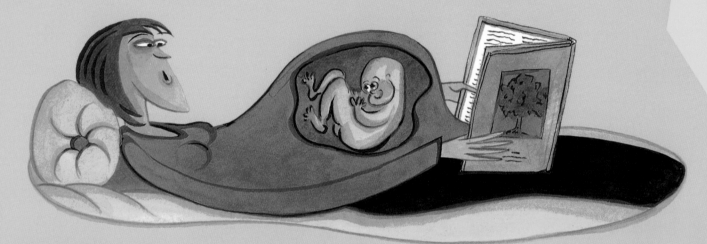

Nature's Headstart

Put your finger next to a newborn baby's face and she'll grab hold. Or place her in a pool of water and her lungs will seal out the water, protecting her from drowning. These responses and others like them are called reflexes — actions that a person carries out automatically.

Everyone has reflexes. They're what make you close your eyes when something comes at them or make you sneeze to clear your nose. Reflexes are built into the baby before she's born. They're nature's way of helping her survive until she can learn to do some things for herself.

- Your brain weighed between 350 and 400 g (12 and 14 oz.) when you were born, but tripled in size before your first birthday. By the time you were in kindergarten, your brain was almost its full adult size of about 1350 g (3 lb.).

- Stegosaurus probably wasn't the brightest dinosaur. At 9 m (30 ft.) long and about 2 t (2 tn.), it was huge, but its brain — at 75 g (3 oz.) — was as puny as a chicken's egg.

Control Yourself

A baby can't control his emotions. If he's angry, sad or happy, he shows it. Gradually he'll learn to think before he acts — keeping his cool instead of losing his temper, or not crying at school to avoid embarrassment.

Scientists have found a strong link between intelligence and the ability to control emotions. Researchers tested four-year-olds by offering each of them a marshmallow. They told each child that she could eat the treat, but she'd get two if she could wait 15 minutes without eating. Only some of the children managed to wait and get the two treats. The others gobbled up the single marshmallow.

The four-year-olds who managed to hold out had more of what's called emotional intelligence. When tested later in life, they got higher grades than the children who couldn't wait.

A Head for Learning

What makes you smarter than a chicken, a dog or any other kind of animal? The way your brain is structured. Neurologists, or people who study the brain, divide it into white matter and gray matter. White matter is the lumpy central core of the brain that connects all the parts together. The gray matter, or cortex, is a 0.5 cm (¼ in.) thick layer of tissue that completely covers the white matter.

Imagine that your white matter is a head of cauliflower and the gray matter is a sauce poured over it. The layer of sauce may be thin, but there has to be lots of it to coat all of the cauliflower's crevasses and indentations. Experts suspect that it's our large amount of gray matter, which contains all of our brain cells, or neurons, that makes us so intelligent.

You have about 100 billion neurons — 10 million times more than the number of stars you can see in a dark, cloudless sky. As you read these words, your eyes send the images of the letters to the part of your brain that deals with language. It figures out what the words mean.

The meaning then gets passed along, from one neuron to the next, to other parts of your brain—the parts that understand the information and store it away in your memory. Each neuron can connect to thousands of other neurons. Through those connections, a message can travel on many different pathways.

Ever noticed how you get better at a skateboarding trick each time you do it? Neurologists think that the first few times you try something new, your brain tests out different pathways of connections through your neurons, finding the best one. Doing the trick over and over makes that pathway stronger, so your skill improves.

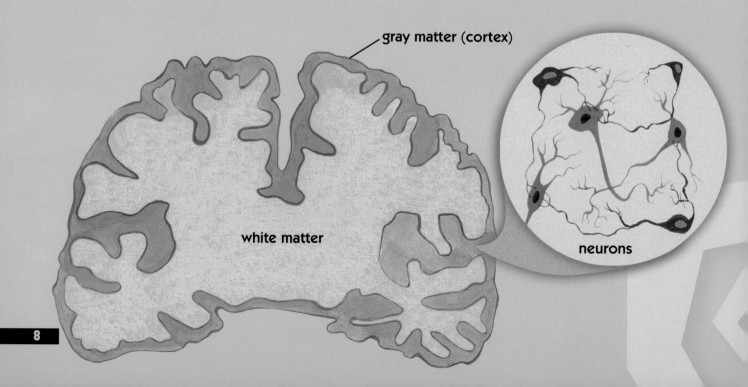

gray matter (cortex)

white matter

neurons

- Don't ask a fish to do your homework. Fish have no frontal lobe or gray matter.

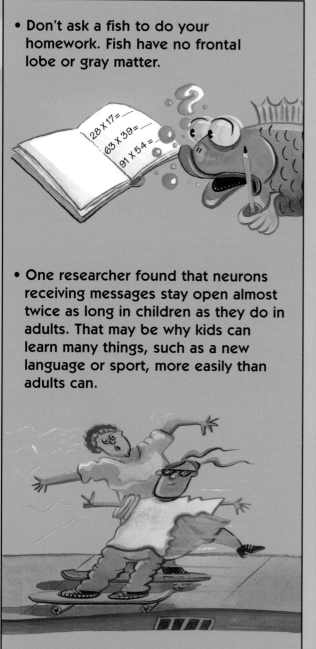

- One researcher found that neurons receiving messages stay open almost twice as long in children as they do in adults. That may be why kids can learn many things, such as a new language or sport, more easily than adults can.

- It would take 32 million years to count, at a rate of one per second, the connections between your neurons.

Love That Lobe

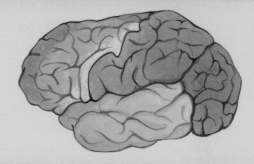

Your brain has four main areas, called lobes, that do different jobs. Your frontal lobe—the biggest chunk—is located right behind your forehead. It's this lobe that does much of the intelligent, complicated work, such as planning and problem solving. Many other animals that we think of as intelligent, monkeys for instance, have large frontal lobes, too.

The foreheads of prehistoric human ancestors didn't rise straight up like yours but instead sloped back. That may mean those early people had much smaller frontal lobes, which could explain why they weren't as smart as people today.

modern

prehistoric

Are You in Your "Right" Mind?

During a war in Europe in 1870, two army doctors did more than just treat injured soldiers. The two men were fascinated by the human brain and wanted to learn which parts did what jobs. Whenever they found a wounded soldier whose brain was exposed, they would stimulate areas of it with mild and painless electric currents.

When the doctors touched areas on the RIGHT side of the brain, it affected the LEFT side of the patient's body, and vice versa. Each half of the brain controlled the opposite half of the body. The experiments taught brain researchers a lot about how the two halves of the brain are different. Those differences may have a lot to do with how we think and learn.

Your brain is divided into two halves that communicate through the corpus callosum, a thick connecting band of 250 million nerve fibers. Though they work together, each half, or hemisphere, is better at different tasks. The left side is hard at work as you write a letter, solve a math question or tackle a word puzzle. The right hemisphere is busy when you sing songs or paint pictures, and it keeps you from getting lost.

• Most people use both brain hemispheres equally. Some psychologists — people who study how we think — believe that people may have one hemisphere that's stronger than the other. That's called brain-dominance. Here are some ways it may affect how a person thinks and learns:

ABCs
123s

Left-Brain Dominant
• uses words to express ideas
• makes lists; follows ordered directions
• links small details to grasp the whole idea
• works well with symbols — letters, numbers, etc.

Right-Brain Dominant
• has trouble expressing ideas in words
• prefers not to follow a set order
• sees the whole idea before the details
• prefers real objects over symbols

You Try It

These questions may give you an idea of whether one side of your brain is dominant over the other, especially when it comes to using your body.

1. Which hand holds the toothbrush as you brush your teeth? Which hand throws a ball?

2. Which foot do you use to kick a ball? Which foot do you lift first when climbing stairs?

3. When you take a picture, which eye do you put to the camera?

4. Turn on a TV or radio with the volume very low. Which ear do you turn toward the TV or radio to better hear whoever's talking?

Some people don't have a dominant hemisphere—they use both sides equally. If you used your right hand, foot, eye or ear, the left side of your brain may be dominant. If you used your left hand, foot, eye or ear, your right hemisphere may be stronger. But not all left-handed people are right-brain dominant. About two-thirds have brains like typical right-handed people.

A Learning Experience

People learn things in many different ways. When you were a preschooler, you probably pretended to do things you'd seen adults do, such as drive a car or wash dishes. Your playing helped you learn a little about those activities.

One method of learning is called trial and error—trying something to see if it works, then trying something else if it doesn't. You'll use this technique your whole life to learn which way to turn the key in a lock, how to fit everything in your backpack and many other things.

Luckily for you, your brain is smart enough to know that information about one task might also work for another. Knowing how to hold a spoon may have helped you learn to hold a pencil, for instance. And once you'd spilled your first few glasses of milk, your brain used reasoning to figure out that you had to carry ANY open container—a box of blocks, a bowl of snacks—with the opening facing up.

The Ways We Learn

People use many different methods of learning all the time. As a teacher teaches, you learn from what he is saying and also from how he is saying it. His gestures and the expressions on his face help you understand.

Learning through words — by reading information or hearing it explained — is called auditory learning. Learning by seeing information — either in pictures or acted out in front of you — is called visual learning. You use both these learning skills, as well as others, all the time. For some tasks you may prefer words, and for others, you may prefer visual clues. As children grow up, most begin to prefer either auditory or visual information.

What you prefer can make a difference in how you learn. One person may prefer to read a new story to learn it. Another would rather see it as a play.

You Try It

Everyone uses both auditory and visual skills all the time. Answer these questions to find out which skills you prefer to use in these situations.

1. If you can choose how you will present a school project, do you prefer to
   a) write a report?
   b) draw a poster?

2. When you learn a new computer game, do you find it easier to
   a) carefully read the rules and follow the instructions?
   b) watch a friend play and imitate her actions?

3. Which would you rather do to tell someone how to get to your school?
   a) give written instructions
   b) draw a map

If you chose the first option for two or three of the questions, you prefer learning these types of information with your auditory skills. If you most often chose the second option, you prefer to use your visual skills for these tasks.

The Perfect Time to Learn

Over 200 years ago, in 1797, some people in Aveyron, France, discovered a naked boy living in the woods beyond the edge of their village. He looked about 12 years old, but he did not speak, preferred to sleep on the floor and behaved very strangely.

Judging by what he chose to eat, the snarling sounds he made and the scars on his body, the people of the village decided he must have been raised by animals. They named him Victor, though most people today call him the Wild Boy of Aveyron.

A doctor tried for years to teach the boy to speak, but Victor only ever learned a handful of words. People decided he must be mentally handicapped. Now experts think he couldn't speak because his best time for learning language had passed. The right time had come when Victor was alone in the woods with no one to listen to except the animals.

- Most people learn 45 000 words between the age of one and the end of high school. That's an average of seven new words every day.

- Dolphins, orangutans and chimpanzees are the only other animals that can recognize themselves in a mirror the way human babies can by the time they're 18 months old. All other creatures think their reflection is another animal.

Ages and Learning Stages

Most babies learn to do things such as smile or roll over by a specific age. Doctors can compare what one baby has learned with what other babies that same age have learned. If a baby has learned many of the same things as other babies, the doctor can be fairly sure that that baby's brain is developing normally.

By the age of	Most babies have begun to
1–2 months	hold up their own heads
6 weeks	smile on purpose
2 months	babble and coo
3–4 months	roll from tummy onto back
5 months	take hold of an object
6–8 months	sit up by themselves
9 months	crawl
10 months	clap their hands
18 months	recognize themselves in the mirror

An adult who didn't learn how to swim or to ride a bike as a child can still learn those things as an adult. But learning language for the first time is different. The human brain seems programmed to learn speech by the age of seven. A child who hasn't learned to speak by then may never be able to learn any language. It's as though the brain moves on to other things and can't go back.

Learning Disabilities

Barbara Arrowsmith wasn't an average child. She got lost constantly and misplaced things. Arrowsmith couldn't even figure out where her own arms and legs were if she couldn't see them! She tripped often and couldn't hold a glass of water in her left hand without spilling it.

That wasn't all. Arrowsmith had great trouble recognizing symbols and understanding how they worked together, so she couldn't tell time. She found grammar impossible. Luckily, even as a young girl she could memorize pages and pages of facts. Thanks to her incredible memory, Arrowsmith made it to university, where she learned more about the problems she had with understanding and learning.

Arrowsmith taught her brain to think in new ways, strengthening parts that were weak. In 1980, she started a school for children with problems like those she'd overcome—problems that make it difficult to learn.

Although every person's brain is different, many people are similar in how they learn. Schools, teaching methods, textbooks—all are designed to work best for those people. Some people, however, learn differently. They have what's called a learning disability.

Learning disabilities can affect how people take in information, how they remember it, how they make sense of it or how they express it. Different disabilities may make it hard for a person to talk and listen, do math, learn to read or spell. Having a learning disability doesn't mean a person is less smart. It just means he needs to be taught in a different way.

Scrambled Letters

As you read this, your brain is doing complicated work. You've heard the word "brain" and know what it means. But to write that word, or any word, you have to break it down into its separate sounds: b-r-ai-n. Then, to read it, you have to turn the letters and their separate sounds back into the word.

For the millions of people with a learning disability called dyslexia (diss-LEK-see-yuh), matching the letters in words to their sounds is extremely difficult. Experts haven't quite figured out why, but they do know that people with dyslexia use different parts of the brain when they read than people without the disability. Luckily, with special training most people with dyslexia can learn to read and write as well as anyone.

Out of Focus

Your brain had to learn how to stay focused on one thing at a time. People with Attention Deficit/Hyperactivity Disorder (AD/HD) have trouble with that. Even if they can decide what needs their attention, they may be distracted before they finish it.

All children struggle with controlling their impulses and paying attention. But kids with AD/HD have differences in the chemicals in their brains that make it much more difficult for them to sit quietly and focus on a task.

Measuring Up

How do you measure someone's "smarts"? Most people talk about "intelligence quotient," or IQ, when they talk about how intelligent a person is. What IQ tests really measure is how smart you are compared with an average person your age.

To find out your IQ, you first answer a long list of IQ questions for your age group. If, for example, you get as many right as most 11-year-olds, 11 is your "mental age." Then you divide your mental age by your real age and multiply by 100. So, if you're really 10, your score would be 11 ÷ 10 × 100, or 110. Experts say that a score between 85 and 115 is average.

Many people say IQ tests aren't perfect. They believe it's impossible for any test to measure ALL the ways a person can be intelligent. Some argue that people from a different culture than those who designed the test may choose answers that are considered wrong, even though those answers make more sense in that particular culture.

Still, IQ tests can be useful for parents and teachers who are trying to figure out what grade a child should be in or what level of schoolwork she should be doing. For other people, IQ is a matter of pride. Organizations, such as Mensa, exist so that members with high IQs can talk together about issues. And they won't let you join unless your IQ score is good enough!

- **Researchers are now measuring the speed of electrical transmissions in a person's brain to measure intelligence. They say that the faster the brain signals, the smarter the person is.**

- **Most adults have the same IQ as they did when they were about eight years old. They've learned more, but how they compare with other people their age is about the same as it was.**

IQ Meter

You Try It

Here are just a few questions that are like those you'd find on an IQ test for 9- to 12-year-olds. You'd have to answer many more to find out your IQ.

1. Three ships are docked side by side. A blue ship is to the right of a red ship and to the left of a green ship. If the blue ship and the green ship change places, which ship ends up in the middle?

2. Which picture goes in the empty box to complete this sequence?

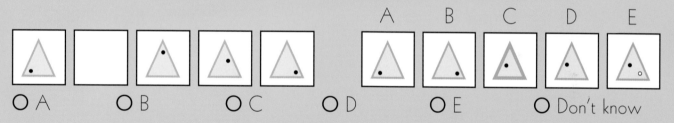

○ A   ○ B   ○ C   ○ D   ○ E   ○ Don't know

3. Your watch is 6 minutes fast, and the train that was due at your station at 11:30 A.M. was 5 minutes late. What time did your watch show when the train arrived?

11:40   11:41   11:38   11:44   11:39

4. These three shapes are similar in some way. Which two shapes from the group on the right are also similar?

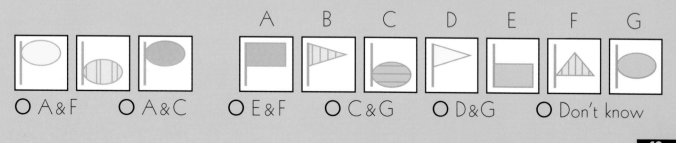

○ A & F   ○ A & C   ○ E & F   ○ C & G   ○ D & G   ○ Don't know

(See page 40 for the answers)

What a Genius!

Ask people to name a genius—someone who's exceptionally intelligent—and most will pick Albert Einstein. Many people consider Einstein the most important scientist of the 20th century. His work in a field called quantum physics changed nearly everything scientists believed about light, time and space. His famous theory of relativity is so complex that many renowned scientists didn't even understand it at first.

Einstein is probably the most famous genius, but there have been many others. Maria Gaetana Agnesi was born in Italy in 1718, the eldest daughter in a family of 21 children. When she was 20, Agnesi began writing a textbook to help her brothers and sisters with their math. She became very serious about the project and had the book published.

Math experts of that time were astonished at how good Agnesi's book was. One university sent her a diploma and immediately asked her to become part of its teaching staff. Her work was translated into other languages and widely used as a textbook.

Not all geniuses are mathematicians. Writers, scientists, musicians and others have all been geniuses. Marie Curie, famous for her work with radioactivity and the element radium, is the only person to win the Nobel Prize in the two separate sciences of physics and chemistry.

Leonardo da Vinci was what's called a "universal genius"—someone who seems to be smart in many different subjects. Da Vinci is as famous for his science and inventions as he is for his works of art.

- Technically, a genius is someone whose IQ is greater than 135. The highest score most IQ tests can accurately measure is about 200.

- How smart you are may not be as important as what you do with your intelligence. Experts think Einstein's IQ may have been about 160. There are people with much higher IQs who haven't made any important discoveries.

- Having a high IQ can often lead to success. Bill Gates, software designer and one of the world's richest people, is estimated to have an IQ of 160.

Einstein's Brain

Is a genius's brain different from your brain? Scientists have studied Einstein's brain, trying to figure out whether there is something about its structure that made him smarter than most people.

What they've found so far is that Einstein's brain didn't weigh any more than the average man's brain. But it was 15 percent wider in the areas used for the kind of mathematical and space-related reasoning Einstein did. As well, the groove that runs from the front to the back of most brains was smaller in Einstein's.

It could be that these features gave Einstein's brain better connections in these areas and that's what made him brilliant in his field. The researchers can't really be sure, however, until they get a chance to study the brains of some other mathematical geniuses and see whether they have these same distinct features.

Smart Kids

Musician Wolfgang Amadeus Mozart learned to play his first piece of classical music on the harpsichord in just half an hour … when he was not quite 5 years old. A few months later, he started composing bits of his own music. At the age of 9, he composed a symphony for a full orchestra of instruments.

There have been many other exceptional children. Some were musicians like Mozart. Others were chess grand masters. Still others graduated from university when they were only 15 or 16. Experts call these children prodigies — kids who perform as well in very challenging fields as highly trained adults.

Most prodigies still act like average kids in every way except their one exceptional skill. No one knows exactly what makes a prodigy, although they all have incredible talent and are very determined to develop it.

Like Mozart, some prodigies continue to astound people as they grow up. Many more don't. For some reason researchers can't yet explain, most prodigies find that their abilities don't increase as quickly as those of other children around them. The others eventually catch up, and the prodigy has to accept the difficult fact that he's no longer special.

- When she was just 4 years old, Chinese artist Wang Yani painted a watercolor picture that was reproduced as a postage stamp. By the time she was 6, her work was being exhibited throughout Europe.

- In 1999, 8-year-old British chess prodigy David Howell became the youngest person ever to win a game of chess against a grand master.

- People used to think scientists would find a handful of genes that make one person smarter than another. It turns out intelligence may involve as many as 150 different genes.

The Power of Young Brains

In some ways, kids have more "brainpower" than their parents. Newborn babies have just as many neurons as adults, but the neurons have almost no connections among them. Once those connections start forming, the number of them increases quickly.

By the time you were 2 years old, your brain had twice as many connections as an adult's. And the brain keeps producing new connections until you're about age 11, when it starts to slow down.

Even though each connection COULD make you smarter, your brain can't look after them all. The ones that don't get used often just kind of fade out.

Good thing, too. Your brain needs clear, distinct paths to get those thoughts where they're going quickly. If your brain kept all those pathways, you'd be very slow at everything.

Too Smart?

William James Sidis was born on April Fool's Day, 1898, but he was no fool. Sidis spoke his first word when he was just 6 months old. By 18 months he could count and read. Before he started school at age 6, he'd learned six languages, including Greek and Latin.

Sidis finished elementary school in just seven months, then completed four years' worth of high school in the next six weeks. He was a university professor by the age of 17.

Many people say Sidis was one of the most brilliant people ever, but perhaps he was too smart for his own good. He didn't know how to get along with others. People made fun of him, and news reporters always looked for his mistakes. No one ever took him seriously. In a world of normal people, Sidis was too different to be understood.

- At the age of 21, Ervin Nyiregyhazi, a piano prodigy who lived about 100 years ago, still couldn't tie his shoelaces. He'd never taken the time away from music to learn!

The Price of Genius?

What do author Virginia Woolf, composer Ludwig van Beethoven and artist Michelangelo have in common? All were brilliant in their fields and all suffered, experts think, from mental illness — a disorder of the mind that affects a person's behavior.

Researchers have discovered that the personalities of creative people are similar to the personalities of people with bipolar disorder, a mental illness that causes quick mood swings from very happy to extremely sad. Perhaps creative people experience the same extremes of emotion, which may also help them be more creative. It's hard to say until more research is done.

Islands of Genius

In 1966, a doctor visited 26-year-old twins in a state hospital. The two men had autism, a brain disorder that makes it hard to relate to people and the world. The twins were famous for their incredible math abilities, although neither one could even add or subtract.

During the doctor's visit, a box of matches spilled on the floor. Instantly, both twins yelled "111!" Then they repeated the number "37" three times. The doctor counted the matches. There were exactly 111 — three groups of 37. He asked how they'd counted the matches so quickly. One twin replied, "We didn't count them. We SAW the 111." They also "saw" three equal groups of 37 matches, even though they didn't understand division.

The twins belonged to a fascinating group of people with savant syndrome. All of them have low general intelligence but one incredible ability — an "island of genius." They are artists, musicians or number experts. Many are autistic.

No one can explain savants' amazing abilities. Some think the savant's brain isn't distracted by all the aspects of life other people deal with. Instead, it focuses on one thing, and that becomes the savant's particular skill.

Other Kinds of Smarts

In 1975, a golf legend was born. Tiger Woods could swing a golf club before he could walk. When he was just three, he played nine holes of golf and scored an incredible 48, a little better than the average adult golfer. Many years and practice swings later, Woods burst onto the golf scene.

As an amateur, Woods won championship titles every year from 1991 to 1996, when he turned pro. In 1997, he played in his first "major" championship tournament as a professional golfer — and won it by a record-breaking 12 strokes. Experts say the speed and accuracy of Woods's swing are closer to perfect than any other golfer's swing.

Tiger, hockey's Wayne Gretzky, tennis star Venus Williams — all are unbelievably excellent at their sport. They can see in their minds what action they need to take and translate that command perfectly to their muscles. It takes a genius level of intelligence to do that. Not the paper-and-pencil kind of genius, but another type — physical genius.

Multiple Intelligences

So, you're not great at math. Does that mean you're not intelligent? No way! Many experts agree that there are many ways to be intelligent.

Someone who is good with movement, as Tiger Woods is, has high bodily/kinesthetic intelligence. There's musical intelligence and logical/mathematical intelligence. If you have linguistic intelligence, you're good with words and language. Spatial intelligence means you're good with pictures and with picturing things in your mind.

Interpersonal intelligence helps you understand other people's feelings. And intrapersonal intelligence means you're good at recognizing your own feelings. People with natural intelligence have a way of recognizing and understanding the patterns in nature.

With all these different ways to be smart, it's not that some people in the world are intelligent and others aren't. It's more likely that you are a unique combination of these intelligences — smart in your own particular way.

You Try It

Everyone is good at some things and not so good at others. Take a look at these lists to see what intelligences you are strong in.

Spatial
- Creating puzzles
- Sketching
- Building things
- Reading maps

Linguistic
- Telling stories
- Writing
- Explaining
- Telling jokes

Logical/Mathematical
- Solving problems
- Collecting things
- Working with shapes
- Experimenting

Bodily/Kinesthetic
- Dancing
- Acting
- Playing sports
- Making crafts

Musical
- Singing/whistling
- Listening to music
- Playing instruments
- Remembering songs

Interpersonal
- Listening to others
- Helping people
- Resolving conflicts
- Making friends

Intrapersonal
- Knowing your strengths
- Sorting out your feelings
- Knowing how you think
- Recognizing your weaknesses

Making the Most of Your Smarts

A few years ago, some researchers discovered that the patterns of electricity flowing through the brain had a lot in common with music. Then the researchers found that rats could find their way through mazes faster after listening to music composed by Mozart.

The researchers announced that listening to music composed by Mozart could make people smarter. Mozart's music began selling like crazy—until more research was done. Those experiments showed that listening to Mozart may help people complete certain tests, but the improvement fades after 15 minutes.

Scientists have figured out that how smart you are depends on both your genes—which pass along your potential for intelligence from your parents—and your experiences. How intelligent you COULD be is decided before you're born, but how intelligent you actually BECOME depends on how hard you work your brain.

- In ancient times, people believed you could learn what another person knew by eating that person's brain. That's why warriors sometimes ate the brains of enemies they'd defeated.

- The IQs of identical twins can be very similar, but they're almost never identical. Although these twins have genes that match exactly and they live in the same environment, they still have different experiences that shape their minds.

Intelligence Boosters?

Many adults take special mixtures of vitamins and other pills, such as ginseng and gingko biloba. They say these substances make them smarter, but scientists haven't yet proved it. Don't try these "smart foods" yourself—they can be harmful to kids.

As far as natural foods go, tests have shown that salmon and other ocean fish contain a good kind of fat that can keep your brain cells healthy. Blueberries may also be a natural brain booster. In experiments, researchers fed the nutrients from blueberries to aging rats and found that they did better at navigating mazes than rats that got a regular diet.

There are also things you should avoid if you want to stay smart. Experts say people who smoke have less oxygen in their blood. Since your brain needs oxygen to function well, smokers may not be as smart as they could be. And drinking alcohol kills brain cells, leaving fewer to do a person's thinking. Staying up late a few nights in a row can also make it hard to think straight during the day.

You Try It

Kids who skip breakfast or don't eat enough good foods, such as fruits, raw vegetables and protein, don't do as well at school as kids who get the right things to eat. For two weeks, try cutting out junk food and soda pop. Instead, eat lots of fruits and vegetables every day. Get plenty of sleep, eat a good breakfast each morning and drink milk. At the end of two weeks, see how you feel. Even if you don't feel smarter, you'll probably feel healthier!

Use It or Lose It

A mother and father bring their three-week-old baby to the hospital. She was born with a cataract—the coating at the front of her left eye is cloudy instead of clear. Her doctors know that if they don't remove the cataract now, the baby will never see normally.

The baby's brain is busy forming connections between its neurons. If one eye doesn't let in much light, her brain won't form the strong connections it needs to pass images from that eye to the brain. Instead, the connections from the strong eye will take over most of the visual part of the brain, while the left-eye connections will shrivel up. Then the baby's brain won't ever be able to process images from that weaker eye, even if the cataract is removed when she's older.

Like muscles, brain pathways need to be exercised to stay useful. Young or old, the more a person uses her brain—by doing puzzles, solving math problems or reading about new subjects—the smarter she gets. Some people call brain exercises that maintain your pathways "neurobics." It's all about keeping your mind challenged.

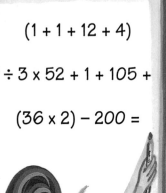

$$(1 + 1 + 12 + 4)$$
$$\div\ 3 \times 52 + 1 + 105 +$$
$$(36 \times 2) - 200 =$$

- **Going to school keeps your mind in shape. Tests show that kids' IQs drop by a point or two over summer holidays and then perk up again when the kids get back to the books.**

The Nun Study

Since 1986, a scientist has been studying 678 retired nuns. He has interviewed them all, studied their pasts and tested their mental skills. He's even dissected the brains of some who've died. All of this is helping him learn about Alzheimer's, a disease that shrinks and damages the brain, robbing older people of their memories and their intelligence.

Scientists know that having certain genes can make a person more apt to get Alzheimer's, but they don't know why some people with those genes get the disease and others don't. The nun research shows that people with a college or university education who keep their minds busy are less likely to get the disease.

How people use language can also give a clue as to who is more at risk. The researcher studied stories the nuns had written 50 years earlier. The women who'd written in complex sentences, packing more ideas into each one, were less likely to develop Alzheimer's in old age than those who wrote in simple sentences.

Whether you're 9 or 90, these exercises can give your mind a workout.

- Brush your teeth or eat with your weaker hand.

- Play cards and word games such as Scrabble.

- Get dressed with your eyes closed.

- Turn this book around and try to read the next page upside down.

31

Starting Over

When Michael Rehbein was seven years old, he was having 300 to 400 seizures almost every day. All of them started in the left hemisphere of his brain. So doctors removed the whole left hemisphere. It's a drastic step, but for some children with brain conditions that cause so many seizures, it's their only hope of living a normal life.

Of course, removing nearly half of a person's brain causes problems. Rehbein's seizures stopped, but the right side of his body — the side his left hemisphere had controlled — was practically paralyzed. Rehbein had to retrain his body to walk, jump and move in all the ways he'd been able to before. As well, the left hemisphere contains the areas used to understand language and to speak. After the surgery, Rehbein had to learn to talk all over again.

Luckily, the brain can adapt, especially in children and teenagers. When one part is removed, other parts can learn to take over. The brain can't do this all on its own, though. That's why physical therapy and rehabilitation are so important. Rehbein had to keep trying an activity to help his brain hook up its new wiring and make it work as well as it could.

An adult who's had a stroke — a broken or blocked blood vessel in the brain — often suffers damage to parts of her brain. Like younger people, she can probably recover some of those lost abilities through therapy and relearning. It's harder than for a child's brain and the progress is slower, but an older brain can still adapt a certain amount.

Whole brain

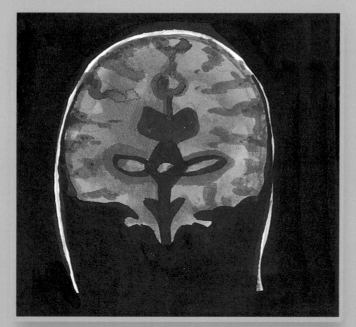

Brain with left hemisphere removed

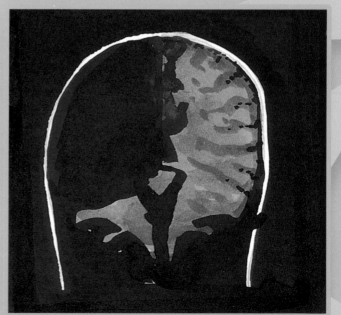

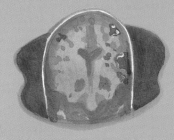

- PET scans show that the more you practice an activity, the less brainpower it requires. An experiment showed fewer areas of the brain lighting up as volunteers got better and better at the video game they were playing.

Having Your Head Examined

In the past, doctors had almost no way of figuring out what was happening inside the brain. It's hard to get a good look at something that's surrounded by bone. When the computerized tomography and computerized axial tomography scans—CT and CAT scans—were invented, doctors could finally take X ray—type pictures inside the skull to find tumors, brain damage or weak blood vessels. Still, they had almost no way of learning what parts of the brain did what jobs.

All that changed with the invention of positron emission tomography, or PET scans, and later functional magnetic resonance imaging (fMRI). Both of these techniques produce snapshots of the brain in action. They can track where blood is flowing—the more blood that flows to an area, the more work that area is doing.

Doctors watching the images can see where more blood flows as the patient reads, speaks and answers math questions, and can figure out what brain areas are involved in those activities.

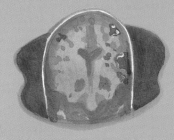

Searching for Intelligence

Since about 1960, a group of scientists has been listening for signals from other planets. They figure since earthlings can send messages into space, someone out there may be trying to send signals back.

In 1999, the scientists realized their computers couldn't analyze all the space "noise" that might contain a signal. They asked the public for help. People could sign up to download some data, and when they weren't using their computer, it would analyze that data and return it to the researchers. By July 2002, nearly 4 million people from 226 countries were taking part.

Intelligence is important to humans. Scientists are also interested in whether other earthly creatures might be able to think as well as humans do. For years, researchers have studied many animals to test their intelligence. Is there anyone out there who's smarter than humans?

If We Could Talk to the Animals

In 1972, a researcher began teaching sign language to a 1-year-old gorilla named Koko. In two weeks, Koko had learned the correct hand signs for "food," "drink" and other words. By the time Koko was 31 years old, she knew more than 1000 signs.

Tests show that Koko's IQ is somewhere between 70 and 95 on a test designed for young children. She's learned some language, but she'll never be as good at putting words together as most older children are.

Does that mean gorillas aren't as smart as people? Maybe it just means their brains aren't wired for language. Language is extremely important to humans. That's why it's used to measure intelligence. But if people had to survive in the jungle, would language still be as important? Gorillas and other animals probably have a lot more survival smarts than you do because THAT'S what matters in the wild.

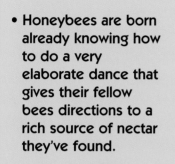

- Honeybees are born already knowing how to do a very elaborate dance that gives their fellow bees directions to a rich source of nectar they've found.

You Try It

See if your dog can pass this intelligence test.

1. Put your dog's favorite treat on the floor and let her sniff it. While she's watching, cover the treat with a clean, empty soup can.

2. Encourage your dog to get the treat. How long does it take her?

5 seconds or less = 5
6—15 seconds = 4
16—30 seconds = 3
31—60 seconds = 2
tries, gives up = 1
doesn't try = 0

3. Put another treat on the floor. Let your dog sniff it. Then throw a dishtowel over it. Time how long it takes your dog to get the treat.

15 seconds or less = 5
16—30 seconds = 4
31—60 seconds = 3
61—120 seconds = 2
tries, gives up = 1
doesn't try = 0

If your dog's total score is 5 or more, she has above-average intelligence!

Building a "Brain"

In 1984, a computer programmer began to design a new kind of software. He wanted to build a program that contained all the general knowledge a typical person learns. He and his team created the program, called Cyc (sike), and they've been feeding it information ever since. They've taught it facts such as "most birds fly" and "if you're carrying a container with an opening, that opening should face up or you'll spill what's inside."

By July 2002, Cyc held about 1.5 million commonsense "rules" about life on Earth, and more were added every day. But it still wasn't smarter than you. For example, Cyc concluded that everyone born before 1900 was famous, because the only people from that era that it had learned about were the famous ones.

Computers vs. Humans

Computers are incredible at certain tasks. Programmed with the right software, they can do complicated math, write poetry and even compose music. Unlike forgetful human brains, they remember things forever. Today's really advanced computers can even learn from experience — they can use what they already know to help them understand something new. But there are still things computers can't do.

Computers with programs that let them see can't recognize and name the objects they are looking at. And "hearing" computers can't learn by listening to someone talk, the way you can, because they don't understand the meaning of the words. As well, these computers can't watch television and understand what's going on or guess what might happen next.

The most powerful computer programs can do one thing — such as identify faces in a crowd, analyze numbers or recognize voices — extremely well. They can do that one thing better than any person, but they can't do any of the dozens of other things a person can do.

If developers one day connect the Cyc software and all its knowledge to a robot with software that lets it see, smell, touch, hear, talk and walk, they might create something that could do most of what you can do. But would this machine be as intelligent as a human being? Until we can figure out exactly what "intelligence" really is, no one knows for sure.

- In 1997, a computer beat world chess champion Garry Kasparov in a six-game chess match. Of course, at 1.4 t (1.5 tn.), its "thinking machine" was a fair bit bigger than Kasparov's 1400 g (3 lb.) brain.

- Many people agree that a good sense of humor is a sign of high intelligence.

What a Computer Can't Do

You're smarter than the most powerful computer that exists today. It can't do any of these things:

- Choose a favorite song.
- Tell someone what this book is about.
- Write a story about what happened today.
- Explain the plot of a movie.
- Make up a funny joke.

Smarter People?

A scientist in New Zealand says you may be smarter than your parents. Or at least, smarter than they were at your age. He's discovered that, compared with 50 years ago, the average person is answering more questions on an IQ test correctly—enough to increase her IQ score by 15 to 25 points.

Some experts believe it's because of the many ways our lives are getting better. The scores have increased in most countries that have better food and health care than they used to. Newborns in those countries may already be brighter because their mothers were healthier during pregnancy, when those tiny brains were forming. And the babies have good food and health care, too, which helps them do even better.

School is the other major thing that's changed. In the early 1900s, there weren't nearly as many schools. Lots of kids couldn't go to school even if there was one nearby—they had to stay home to help with the farming or look after their brothers and sisters. Now, most people realize that learning makes you smarter, and more kids get the chance to go to school.

You're constantly learning and getting smarter. The more you do and learn, the more intelligent you'll be. In fact, your brain is different now than it was when you began reading this book. You've learned new things and discarded others you don't need. And with a healthy brain, you'll keep doing that your whole life.

- Some experts say humans aren't getting smarter — just better at taking intelligence tests, which only test certain skills.

- Two Australian scientists say they've created a real thinking cap. When people put it on, it uses magnetism to stimulate certain parts of their brain to unlock creative skills they didn't think they had. The scientists claim that 17 volunteers could draw better after wearing the cap for just 15 minutes.

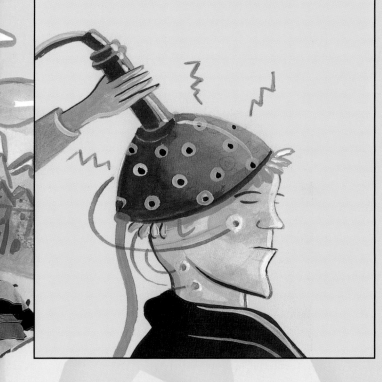

The 10 Percent Myth

Ever heard anyone say that people use only 10 percent of their brains? Imagine how much smarter people would be if they could use the rest. Maybe humans could do amazing things, such as predict the future or move objects with just their minds.

Unfortunately, brain experts say they're not likely to ever come up with a way to turn regular brains into superbrains. Research shows that there is no large, unused part of the brain. People are already using most of their brains all the time. So although you may never have psychic powers, your brain can do everything it needs to, and it'll always have enough room for new information.

Index

activities
    answer IQ questions, 19
    boost intelligence, 29
    exercise your brain, 31
    identify areas of intelligence, 27
    investigate auditory/visual learning, 13
    test a dog's intelligence, 35
    test for brain-dominance, 11
AD/HD, 17
ages for learning, 14–15
Agnesi, Maria Gaetana, 20
alcohol, 29
Alzheimer's, 31
ancestors, 9
animal intelligence, 9, 14, 28, 29, 34, 35
Arrowsmith, Barbara, 16
Attention Deficit/Hyperactivity Disorder, 17
auditory learning, 13
autism, 25

babies, 6, 14, 15, 23, 30
Beethoven, Ludwig van, 24
bipolar disorder, 24
brains, 4, 5, 8, 16, 28, 31, 39
    boosters, 28, 29
    cortex, 8
    dominance, 10–11
    electricity in, 18, 28
    exercises, 30, 31
    hemispheres, 10, 11, 32
    scans, 5, 33
    size of, 7
    structure of, 8, 9, 10, 21, 30

cells, 8. **See also** neurons
chemicals in, 17
chess, 22, 23, 37
child prodigies, 22, 23, 24
computer intelligence, 36, 37
corpus callosum, 10
Curie, Marie, 20

da Vinci, Leonardo, 20

dogs, 35
dyslexia, 17

Einstein, Albert, 20, 21
emotional intelligence, 7

foods, 29
frontal lobe, 9

Gates, Bill, 21
genes, 23, 28, 31
genius, 20–21, 24
    "islands of," 25
    physical, 26, 27
    "universal," 20
gorillas, 34
gray matter, 8, 9
Gretzky, Wayne, 26

Hawking, Stephen, 4
hemispheres of brain, 10, 11, 32
Howell, David, 23

intelligence
    boosters, 28, 29
    different kinds of, 26–27
    emotional, 7
    measuring, 18–19, 34, 35
    of animals, 14, 28, 29, 34, 35
    of computers, 36, 37
    of dogs, 35
    of gorillas, 34
    of kids vs. adults, 9, 15, 22–23, 38
    on other planets, 34
    quotient, 18–19. **See also** IQ
    what it is, 4–5, 36, 37, 39
intelligences, multiple, 26–27
IQ, 18–19, 21, 28, 30, 34

Kasparov, Garry, 37
Koko, 34

language, 8, 14, 15, 31, 32, 34
learning, 6, 12–13, 14–15, 16, 32, 38
    auditory, 13
    disabilities, 16–17
    trial and error, 12
    visual, 13
left, right brain hemispheres, 10, 11, 32
lobe, frontal, 9

measuring intelligence, 18–19, 34, 35
Mensa, 18
mental
    age, 18
    illness, 24
Michelangelo, 24
Mozart, Wolfgang Amadeus, 22, 28
multiple intelligences, 26–27
music, 28

"neurobics," 30
neurologists, 8
neurons, 8, 9, 23, 30
Nyiregyhazi, Ervin, 24

physical genius, 26, 27
prodigies, 22, 23, 24
psychic powers, 39
psychologists, 10

reading, 4, 8, 16, 17
reflexes, 6
Rehbein, Michael, 32
relearning, 32
right, left brain hemispheres, 10, 11, 32

savant syndrome, 25
scans, brain, 5, 33
school, 30, 38
senses, 5
Sidis, William James, 24
sleep, 29
"smart foods," 29
smoking, 29
speech, 14, 15, 32
strokes, 32

thinking caps, 39
twins, 25, 28

visual learning, 13

white matter, 8
Wild Boy of Aveyron, 14
Williams, Venus, 26
Wilson, Charlie, 27
Woods, Tiger, 26
Woolf, Virginia, 24

Yani, Wang, 23

Answers for page 19: 1. green, 2. D, 3. 11:41, 4. C & G